BRITAIN
FROM ABOVE

D0550674

IAN HAY

TEXT: GRAHAM PRITCHARD

MYRIAD
LONDON

LONDON

Britain's capital, its seat of government, a major financial centre and home to the royal family, London is one of the world's greatest cities. Visitors flock here for its remarkable buildings, beautiful parks, ceremonial pageantry and fascinating mix of people. Samuel Johnson's lines written over 200 years ago still ring true today: "When a man is tired of London, he is tired of life; for there is in London all that life can afford."

POOL OF LONDON *right*

The section of the Thames known as the Pool of London flows from Butler's Wharf and St Katherine Docks below Tower Bridge to London Bridge. Either side of this stretch of the river lie landmarks such as the Tower of London (founded in 1078) and Sir Norman Foster's elliptical City Hall, home of the Greater London Authority since 2002. Moored in the river is the museum ship *HMS Belfast*, which saw action during the Second World War. Over 70,000 tons of concrete and 11,000 tons of steel went into the construction of Tower Bridge which began in 1886 and lasted eight years. Since 1974 the bridge's opening mechanism has been electro-hydraulically driven. It opens more than a thousand times a year, and each opening takes just a minute. As the Bridgemaster's Dining Room is now licensed for weddings and civil partnerships, it is possible to get married at Tower Bridge.

BUCKINGHAM PALACE *above*

Buckingham House, the forerunner of today's palace, was bought for Queen Charlotte by George III in 1761 and became known as the Queen's House. Remodelling and enlarging soon began. Three weeks after Victoria came to the throne in 1837 she declared the palace the official London residence of the monarch. In front of the palace stands the white marble Victoria Memorial erected in 1911. Today's Buckingham Palace has 775 rooms. Every year in August and September the 19 State Rooms are open to the public. Spectators flock to see the daily ceremony of the Changing of the Guard in the forecourt.

WHITEHALL *right*

Running between Trafalgar Square and Parliament Square, Whitehall has become synonymous with "the Government". The street is lined with government departments including the Ministry of Defence, the Foreign and Commonwealth Office, the Scottish and Welsh Offices and the Treasury. Every year on Remembrance Sunday members of the royal family join politicians, dignitaries and old soldiers to remember the fallen at the Cenotaph. It bears the simple words "The Glorious Dead". A recent addition to Whitehall, the national monument to the women of the Second World War, was unveiled by the Queen in 2005. Although Henry VIII moved out in 1512, Westminster is still officially a royal palace. The oldest part of today's Houses of Parliament, Westminster Hall, dates from 1097. The present building was designed by Sir Charles Barry and completed in 1870. It is one of the world's largest parliaments, with almost 1,200 rooms, 100 staircases and over 2 miles (3km) of corridors. At the north-eastern end, close to Westminster Bridge, stands the 316ft (96m) tall Clock Tower, better known as Big Ben. This is in fact the name of the largest of the tower's five bells, which chimes every hour.

REGENT STREET (NORTH) *below*

Named after the Prince Regent (who became King George IV in 1820), Regent Street was built by the great architect of London John Nash (1752-1835). He created a masterplan for this part of the town stretching north from Regent Street to Regents Park, and which included elegant terraces, crescents and shopping streets. Upper Regent Street is the home of Broadcasting House, the headquarters of the BBC. The Oxford Circus tube station, where Regent Street crosses Oxford Street, is one of the busiest on the London Underground system.

PICCADILLY CIRCUS *left*

Piccadilly Circus was laid out in 1819 to connect Regent Street with Piccadilly. Some accounts say the name comes from *pickadil*, a type of broad lacy collar, others that it was a round hem or additions to a skirt hem. Away from the streaming traffic, set to one side of Piccadilly Circus, the Shaftesbury Monument memorial fountain commemorates the work of the Victorian philanthropist Lord Shaftesbury. The Angel of Christian Charity statue which graces the fountain is better known as Eros. It was the world's first statue cast in aluminium. The vibrantly illuminated advertising hoardings above shops on the north side have long been a popular tourist attraction, particularly at night.

BRITISH MUSEUM *right*

Every year the British Museum, one of the world's finest, attracts more than 5m visitors. It was established by Act of Parliament in 1753 and first opened its doors in Montagu House in 1759. But a new home was needed to accommodate the growing collections, and between 1823 and 1847 the museum became Europe's largest building site while Sir Robert Smirke's neo-classical building took shape. When the British Library moved to its new purpose-built home in St Pancras in 1998, Smirke's original courtyard was redeveloped. It opened two years later as the Queen Elizabeth II Great Court, surrounding the central Reading Room and designed by Sir Norman Foster. It is the largest covered square in Europe, with a roof made of 1,656 individually shaped glass sections.

ROYAL ALBERT HALL *below*

Queen Victoria opened the Royal Albert Hall of Arts & Sciences in 1871. As with the Albert Memorial, opposite, in Kensington Gardens, it is dedicated to her husband, the Prince Consort. In the past the hall could accommodate audiences of up to 9,000, but modern safety regulations limit the present capacity to 5,544. The venue is home to the BBC Proms, an annual series of summer concerts, and it also hosts many sporting events and pop concerts. When ABBA gave two concerts in 1977, the box office reportedly received 3.5m ticket requests.

ST PAUL'S CATHEDRAL *right*

The Great Fire of London in 1666 destroyed the previous cathedral, and Sir Christopher Wren was brought in to design the fourth to occupy this site. He had been an architect for just three years when it was commissioned. By the time St Paul's was finished he was 35 years older. One of London's greatest landmarks, Wren's splendid cathedral has been used for the funerals of Lord Nelson, the Duke of Wellington and Sir Winston Churchill and in 1981 for the wedding of Prince Charles to Lady Diana Spencer.

SWISS RE BUILDING *left*

Number 30 St Mary Axe has firmly established itself in the hearts of Londoners as the Gherkin. It is also known as the Swiss Re building, after its main tenant, a Swiss reinsurance company. It occupies the site of the former Baltic Exchange, destroyed by an IRA bomb in 1992. Foster and Partners designed it as the city's first environmentally sustainable tower with 40 floors rising 590ft (180m). Those who work in the building and their guests can enjoy superb panoramic views from the tower's top floor bar. The Gherkin has won numerous awards, including the prestigious RIBA Stirling Prize when it opened in 2004. Tower 42 (foreground) takes its shape from the logo of its original tenant, the NatWest Bank. At 600ft (183m) it was the UK's highest building until it was surpassed in 1990 by Canary Wharf down river in Docklands.

CANARY WHARF *above*

At the heart of Canary Wharf sits the UK's tallest inhabited building. Number 1 Canada Square, the 771ft (235m) tower, is better known as Canary Wharf. It was designed by the architect César Pelli and completed in 1991. Its triangular roof can be seen from miles around. In 2002, using only his hands and feet and with no safety equipment, the French urban climber Alain Robert scaled the outside of the building. Flanking Number 1 Canada Square are the UK's joint second highest buildings, both 654ft (199m) tall – Citigroup Centre and 8 Canada Square, also called the HSBC Tower. This group of skyscrapers are located on the Isle of Dogs, a tongue of land situated between Limehouse Reach and North Greenwich. Dockyards and shipyards thrived here from the early 1800s until the mid-20th century.

SOUTH-EAST ENGLAND

For many visitors, the south-east is the first part of the country they see – but it is often glimpsed fleetingly as they speed by car or train towards London. Were they to pause for a while, they would be rewarded with a kaleidoscope of views and experiences. Kent, the oldest county in England, with a proud historical heritage is known as the Garden of England where the white-painted chimneys of oasthouses peek out above sleepy apple orchards. Beautiful Sussex, with its rolling downs, offers traditional seaside fun – but often with a modern touch. And further along the coast, Hampshire's impressive naval heritage contrasts with the New Forest (despite its name, one of the oldest in the country) where the ancient landscape has remained unchanged for almost a thousand years.

WINDSOR CASTLE *above*

For nearly 1,000 years Britain's monarchs have lived at Windsor Castle. It is the oldest and the largest occupied castle in the world. In November 1992 nine of the castle's main rooms were destroyed by fire and many more were damaged. The five-year programme of restoration was partly funded by the opening of parts of Buckingham Palace to the public for the first time. Ten kings lie buried in the castle's St George's Chapel, along with Queen Elizabeth the Queen Mother and Princess Margaret.

HAMPTON COURT *right*

When Thomas Wolsey, later Lord Chancellor and Cardinal, leased Hampton Court Palace on the banks of the Thames in 1514, he set about making it a palace fit for a king. He gifted the palace to Henry VIII in 1525 but four years later he fell from grace after failing to have Henry's marriage to Catherine of Aragon annulled. In 1689 William III commissioned Sir Christopher Wren to redesign the King and Queen's apartments; his magnificent South Wing overlooks the formal gardens. The famous Maze was planted in 1691. After the death of George III, Hampton Court was no longer a royal residence and Queen Victoria opened it to the public in 1838.

DOVER *left*

One of Edward the Confessor's Confederation of Cinque Ports, Dover has been of strategic importance since the Romans knew it as *Portus Dubris*. Cross-Channel traffic really took off with the arrival of the railway in 1844. The most prestigious way to travel between London and Paris in the early 20th century was on the Golden Arrow/*Flèche d'Or* Pullman train. Even today, in the age of the plane, 14m passengers pass through Dover every year, and the port handles over 2m lorries.

CANTERBURY CATHEDRAL

Canterbury is dominated by its cathedral. St Augustine, a missionary from Pope Gregory the Great in Rome, founded it in 597AD. Over the centuries it has been rebuilt in a variety of styles. Henry II appointed his friend Thomas à Becket Archbishop of Canterbury in 1162 but Becket vigorously defended the church against royal intervention. Henry's rage at this "meddlesome priest" prompted four knights to assassinate Becket at the cathedral's altar in 1170. Three years later Becket was declared a saint by the pope. Canterbury's cathedral, St Martin's (England's oldest church) and the ruins of St Augustine's abbey are a World Heritage Site.

BRIGHTON *above*

The little village of *Brighthelmston* was mentioned in the Domesday Book in 1086. Royalty started to visit Brighton during the 18th century, and the Prince Regent (later King George IV) arrived in 1783. His summer residence, the Royal Pavilion, is the extravagant jewel in Brighton's crown. John Nash transformed the original farmhouse with his Indian-inspired design. Day-trippers from London thronged to the resort with the coming of the railway in 1841. Brighton's pebble beach is one of the easiest to reach from the capital and its nickname is London-by-the-Sea. Today Brighton thrives as a centre for conferences and is a magnet for English language students.

PORTSMOUTH *below left*

Most of Portsmouth is located on Portsea Island and it is the UK's only island city. It boasts a population density second only to inner London and a naval heritage second to none. The town was founded by a Norman landowner, John de Gisors, in 1180. Twenty years later a naval base was established and the first docks built. For centuries, English monarchs frequently used the base to attack the French and enhance their naval power. In October 1805 Admiral Horatio Nelson set sail aboard his flagship *HMS Victory* en route for his famous victory over the French and Spanish at the Battle of Trafalgar. Today *Victory* takes pride of place at Portsmouth's Historic Dockyard (right). Built between 1759 and 1765, she is the world's oldest warship still in commission. The Trafalgar Day ceremony on board *HMS Victory* takes place annually on October 21. Near to the *Victory* is the splendid exhibition hall housing the *Mary Rose*, Henry VIII's flagship which sank in 1545 and was raised in 1982. The city celebrated its naval heritage in 2005 with the opening of the 558ft (170m) gleaming white Spinnaker Tower, in the shape of a sail. Southsea Common, facing the sea, has drawn crowds to many a naval celebration, parade and aerial display and friends and relatives throng the quayside when ships of the Royal Navy arrive and depart from the busy naval port.

THE NEEDLES *above*

The distinctive line of three chalk stacks stretch out to sea at the western extremity of the Isle of Wight, close to Alum Bay. The formation takes its name from the fourth needle-shaped pillar which collapsed in a storm in 1764. The last lighthouse-keepers left in 1994 when the lighthouse was automated. In 1897 Guglielmo Marconi sent the first ever wireless transmission from a hotel on the colourful sandy cliffs of Alum Bay. With its mild climate, pretty villages and rugged coastline the Isle of Wight has always attracted visitors. Queen Victoria and Prince Albert would summer at Osborne House, and Charles Dickens, Lewis Carroll and Tennyson all visited the island.

SOUTH-WEST ENGLAND

From Cornwall through Devon to Somerset, Dorset and Avon, the south-west has more than 600 miles of stunning coastline and 14 areas of outstanding natural beauty. So it's no surprise that all through the summer visitors flock to the area to visit such attractions as the stunning Eden Project and relax on the beaches. For walkers there are miles of footpaths and moorland to explore, while "end-to-enders" head straight to Land's End with one thing in mind: to walk or cycle the 874 miles from this southernmost tip of England to the most northerly point at John O'Groats in Scotland. The first person to complete this journey, Robert Carlyle, did it in 1879 pushing a wheelbarrow!

STONEHENGE AND CERNE ABBAS

Take a moment to consider that the early earthworks at Stonehenge (above) date from around 3100BC; that the bluestones were brought 240 miles from south-west Wales to the site in about 2150BC; that the outer ring of sarsen stones, each weighing about 25 tonnes, arrived at Stonehenge about 150 years later –

and there can be no doubt that Stonehenge deserves to be a World Heritage Site. Crowds still gather to celebrate the summer solstice though Stonehenge's original purpose remains a mystery. The earliest written mention of the Cerne Abbas giant (above) dates from 1694, but his origin is unknown. The giant, also known as the Rude Man (meaning "naked man") is 180ft (55m) tall and 167ft (51m) wide, cut into a steep chalk hill north of Dorchester. He carries a 120ft (37m) long knobbly club, and is best seen from across the valley or from the air.

CHESIL BEACH AND PORTLAND HARBOUR

It has been calculated that Chesil Beach (right) is made up of 180bn pebbles! The "tombolo" or shingle bank stretches 18 miles (28km) from Portland west towards West Bay; in parts it is 660ft (200m) wide and 50ft (15m) high. Behind it is the Fleet, a saltwater lagoon. This area is rich in wading birds, and at the Abbotsbury swannery hundreds of nesting mute swans rear their cygnets. At the end of Chesil Beach rises the Isle of Portland, an important naval harbour since Henry VIII's time. The surrounding waters are classed as northern Europe's best by the Royal Yachting Association, so it is no surprise that the National Sailing Academy was established here on the south-western shore. Portland Harbour will stage the sailing events in the 2012 Olympic Games.

TORQUAY *below*

During the Second World War wounded soldiers came to convalesce in Torquay. After the war the resort was promoted as a holiday destination. Today, with its palm-lined promenades, fine beaches and an excellent climate, Torquay lives up to its nickname of the English Riviera. The new marina, lined with popular bars and restaurants, can accommodate 440 boats.

PLYMOUTH *left*

Overlooking Plymouth Sound, one of Europe's largest natural harbours, Plymouth lies at the mouth of the Tamar and Plym rivers. It was one of the main departure points for the allied Normandy Landings in 1944. Today the port has more amicable ferry links with Santander in northern Spain and Roscoff in Brittany. Sir Francis Drake reputedly played bowls on Plymouth Hoe while waiting for the tides and winds to change, prior to defeating the Spanish Armada in 1588.

TAMAR BRIDGES *above*

The river Tamar forms a large part of the border between Devon and Cornwall. It is crossed by 20 bridges. The twin arches of Isambard Kingdom Brunel's Royal Albert Bridge, opened in 1859, carry the railway line across the river. When the Tamar road bridge (behind) opened in 1961 it was the UK's longest suspension bridge. Drivers have to pay a toll only when they leave Cornwall.

EDEN PROJECT *above*

A hit since it opened in 2001, the spectacular Eden Project, the brainchild of Tim Smit, is sited in a former china clay pit near St Austell. The Humid Tropics Biome (foreground) is the world's biggest greenhouse and houses tropical plants. A Mediterranean climate has been created in the smaller Warm Temperate Biome, while the Outdoor Biome is planted with lavender, tea, hops and hemp.

ST IVES *left*

From JMW Turner to Barbara Hepworth, many of Britain's foremost artists have come to St Ives. Its importance in the nation's art scene was acknowledged when the Tate opened a gallery here in 1993. St Ives was named by the *Guardian* newspaper as its seaside town of the year in 2007. Neighbouring Newquay has firmly established itself as Britain's surfing capital. Fistral beach regularly stages major international surfing competitions. Each May Volkswagen and custom car drivers head to Newquay for the "Run to the Sun" music weekend. Looe, on the river Looe, is rated as one of the 10 best places in Britain to celebrate the New Year. More generally the town thrives on tourism and fishing.

BARNSTAPLE *below*

In 2007 the new bypass and elegant five-span bridge to the west of the busy town of Barnstaple was completed, easing congestion in the town centre. Thought to be Britain's oldest borough, Barnstaple, on the banks of the river Taw, has been an important market town and trading centre since the Middle Ages. The Victorian cast-iron and glass Pannier Market houses Butchers Row, 10 shops which date from 1855.

CLIFTON SUSPENSION BRIDGE

When he was just 24, Isambard Kingdom Brunel was commissioned to build the Clifton Suspension Bridge (right). Its construction was dogged by financial and political problems and Brunel died in 1859 before it was finished. The bridge was finally completed in 1864 as a memorial to him. It spans the Avon Gorge 245ft (76m) above the river. Weight restrictions mean only cars and light trucks can cross the bridge now, but 4m vehicles use it every year.

BATH *below*

The Romans were the first to document the UK's only natural hot springs at Bath. Taking the waters was a popular pastime for the wealthy in Elizabethan and Georgian times, when Bath experienced a building boom. The city has no fewer than eight Georgian crescents. Lansdown Crescent was designed by John Palmer and built between 1789 and 1793. From the crescent high on Lansdown Hill there are extensive views over the city centre, including the famous Royal Crescent below. Bath is now a World Heritage Site. The spa itself was closed for nearly 30 years but re-opened to the public in 2006 as the Thermae Bath Spa, with natural thermal baths and a rooftop pool. This beautiful complex provides both traditional and modern spa facilities and allows visitors to benefit from the city's healing waters in a luxurious and up-to-date setting.

CENTRAL ENGLAND

The geographical heart of Britain, central England is also the heart of the country's industrial base and prosperity. This is where the Industrial Revolution was born. By Victorian times the area known as the Black Country to the north and west of Birmingham was the most highly industrialised part of Britain. It is a region of great contrasts. Its vibrant cities include Birmingham, Britain's second largest city, together with Derby, Leicester and Nottingham. To the south-west are the gentle hills and rural rolling landscapes of the Cotswolds, dotted with pretty villages and charming market towns. To complete the mix there are some of Britain's finest stately homes and imposing castles.

BIRMINGHAM *above*

It was not long before the Gravelly Hill Interchange became universally known as Spaghetti Junction. This is junction six on the M6 motorway, where it meets the A38 (M) Aston Expressway and a host of other major and minor roads. It was Britain's first free-flow interchange without roundabouts or traffic lights. Construction started in 1968 and lasted for four years. The junction serves 18 routes and covers approximately 30 acres (12 ha). Five hundred and fifty-nine concrete columns up to 80ft (24.4m) high support the intricate road layout, which straddles three canals, two rivers and a main railway line.

The Bullring started life in 1166 when Birmingham was first granted a charter giving it the right to hold its own market. The enclosed shopping centre that opened in 1964 was as big as 26 football pitches – one of the world's largest outside America. By the 1990s however it was widely disliked and considered a concrete monstrosity. It needed a facelift and, in 2000, a £450m refurbishment began. The result is an amazing glass-covered space with high quality shops. Most innovative is the new curvaceous Selfridges department store designed by Future Systems. The skin of this landmark building is covered by thousands of aluminium disks, making it look like the scales of a snake. The iconic circular Rotunda building survives from the 1960s, as does the historic St Martin's church, keeping watch over St Martin's Square at the heart of the complex.

OXFORD *left*

Oxford's High Street, known locally as The High, carves a broad swathe through Oxford from The Plain to Carfax Tower. This is the poet Matthew Arnold's "city of dreaming spires". Either side of The High lie some of the university's 39 colleges and most important buildings. Behind the University Church of St Mary the Virgin sits the circular Radcliffe Camera, built in 1737 to house the Radcliffe Science Library. Today it is part of the adjacent Bodleian Library, one of the UK's five copyright deposit libraries. Oxford is the oldest university in the English-speaking world. Teaching was underway in 1096 and 100 years later the first foreign student arrived. Today more than 130 nationalities are represented among the 18,000 student body.

NOTTINGHAM *above*

At the heart of the city lies Old Market Square, the largest such square in England. It is dominated by the 200ft (61m) dome of the neo-Baroque Council House. The tower's bell, Little John, has the deepest tone of any bell in the country and on a clear day you can hear it seven miles (11km) away. Nottingham's two football clubs stand on opposite banks of the river Trent. Notts County FC, the oldest professional team in the world, play at the Meadow Lane ground on the north side, and to the south is the City Ground, the home of Nottingham Forest FC, who were once managed by Brian Clough. The famous Trent Bridge cricket ground, where Test match cricket has been played since 1899, lies south of the City Ground in West Bridgford.

WARWICK CASTLE *left*

High above the river Avon perches Warwick Castle, one of England's great treasures. Ethelfleda, daughter of Alfred the Great, is said to have raised the first fortifications in 914AD. The earldom of Warwick is one of the oldest in England. The present shape of the castle, including Caesar's Tower and dungeon and the hexagonal Guy's Tower, dates from the 14th century. The State Rooms were extended a century later in honour of Elizabeth I, the first of several royal visitors. Today the castle is run commercially and attracts tens of thousands of visitors a year. There are jousting tournaments, falconry and even the world's biggest trebuchet, a siege machine that fires 33lb (15kg) stones.

EASTERN ENGLAND

From the mouth of the Thames north to the waters of the Wash and the river Humber, eastern England encompasses the ancient kingdom of East Anglia and the modern county of Lincolnshire. Eastern England has two unique areas of countryside – the Fens and the Norfolk Broads. The coast is blessed with long sand and shingle beaches, fringed by mudflats, saltmarsh and reedbeds, all havens for a remarkable range of wildlife. The coastal areas of North Norfolk and Suffolk contain some of the finest seaside resorts in England. Inland the magnificent cities of Cambridge, Ely, Norwich and Lincoln have a fine heritage of cathedral architecture and splendid ancient buildings. On the coast are the thriving ports of Harwich, Felixstowe, Immingham and Grimsby.

SOUTHEND-ON-SEA *left*

With the advent of the railway, Southend became a popular seaside resort for Londoners. Its iconic pier has survived a number of fires (the last in 2005) as well as the occasional ship crashing into it. At 1.34 miles (2.15km) it is the world's longest pleasure pier, opened in stages between 1889 and 1929. In its heyday in 1949 it attracted 7m visitors.

SIZEWELL *right*

Sizewell on the Suffolk coast is dominated by its two nuclear power stations. Sizewell A (right of picture) was closed at the end of 2006: the decommissioning process will last about 100 years and is forecast to cost an estimated £1.2bn. The white dome at Sizewell B, Britain's only large pressurised water nuclear reactor, houses the outer of the reactor's two containment buildings. Sizewell B produces three per cent of the country's energy needs.

CAMBRIDGE *left*

When students fled from the hostile townsfolk of Oxford in 1209, they set up an alternative seat of learning in Cambridge. This makes it the second oldest university in Britain. Peterhouse, dating from 1284, is the oldest Cambridge college. Women students were only admitted as full members of the university in 1948, and there are still three women-only colleges: Newnham, New Hall and Lucy Cavendish. The foundation stone of King's College Chapel (left) was laid by King Henry VI in 1446, but the impressive building was only completed 69 years later. Today King's College choir delights millions of listeners worldwide on Christmas Eve in the traditional Festival of Nine Lessons and Carols, first broadcast in 1928. The city centre is dominated by many of the university's historic buildings. The School of Pythagoras, one of the first educational establishments in Cambridge, was founded in 1200, and the building still stands in the grounds of St John's College. The famous Backs - the rear parts of those colleges which border the river Cam - is a popular tourist spot where punts can be hired for a trip along the river. These traditional flat-bottomed boats were used widely in the Fens, the marshy low-lying countryside north of Cambridge and were introduced as pleasurecraft to the town in Edwardian times. Cambridge is also famous for its beautiful meadowland which extends into the heart of the city.

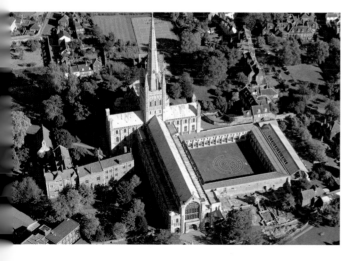

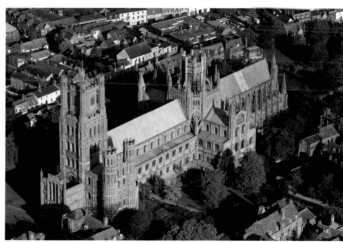

CATHEDRAL CITIES

The great cathedrals of eastern England have been symbols of the Christian faith since the 11th and 12th centuries. Norwich cathedral (above) is famed for its unique two-storey cloisters and its 315ft (96m) tower, the second tallest in England. The roof of the nave is embellished with over one thousand carved bosses that depict Biblical characters and scenes from the lives of the saints. Norwich is one of three cathedrals in England without any bells; the others are the superb Romanesque Ely cathedral (above right) and Salisbury in Wiltshire. Ely cathedral is known locally as "the ship of the Fens" because of its slender tower which looms above the surrounding flat countryside. The Octagon, an eight-sided tower in the centre of the building, is the only Gothic dome in existence. Lincoln cathedral (right) is Britain's third largest and it has the tallest medieval tower in Europe.

KING'S LYNN AND THE WASH *left*

King's Lynn is on the banks of the Great Ouse river, close to where it flows into the Wash and the North Sea. Norfolk meets Lincolnshire at the Wash, where four rivers flow into one of Britain's largest estuaries. The square-shaped Wash and the surrounding low-lying Fens are a wildlife special protection site under EU legislation. The Norfolk Broads were formed by flooding of old peat beds. Since the early 20th century boating on the lock-free waterways has been a popular holiday pastime.

FELIXSTOWE DOCKS *below*

Britain's largest container port, Felixstowe is the fourth largest in Europe after Rotterdam, Hamburg and Antwerp. It is also an attractive seaside resort and is well-known for the extensive and glorious gardens that run the length of the promenade and into the town centre. On the seafront is the Spa Pavilion Theatre, which features ballet, drama and pantomime as well as a modern cinema. At Felixstowe Ferry, part of the old town, there is a ferry across the estuary to Bawdsey.

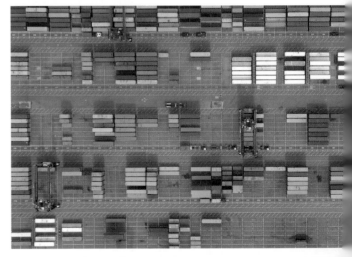

GRIMSBY *right*

Legend has it that Grimsby, on the Humber estuary, was founded in the 9th century by a Danish fisherman called Grim. Its location provided shelter for boats. Over the centuries the town grew into an important trading and fishing port. Six years after the Grimsby Docks Act of 1845 the 309ft (94m) high Dock Tower at the entrance to Royal Dock was completed. With the arrival of refrigeration 100 years later Grimsby was the busiest and largest fishing port in the world. It was here that Birds Eye produced the first fish finger in 1955. Grimsby, together with nearby Immingham, is the UK's largest port in terms of tonnage and in 2006 handled some 57 million tonnes. George V opened Immingham docks in 1913. They are the country's largest deep-sea docks and, with the surrounding industrial facilities, handle large volumes of coal and iron ore, pulp and paper, oil and petro-chemicals from all over the world. There are two refineries (above) at Killingholme, to the west.

YORKSHIRE

England's largest county boasts a diverse landscape which few areas of Britain can match, from the mighty cities of west and south Yorkshire, and the rural charms of the moors and dales to its stunning coastline. The urban regions have a long history of mining and manufacturing and many of the area's landmarks still reflect this industrial past. North Yorkshire has two areas of outstanding natural beauty – the North York Moors and the Yorkshire Dales. The Yorkshire coastline is one of the county's crowning glories. Between the Heritage Coast in the north and Spurn Head in the south are a succession of dramatic bays, glorious beaches and cliffs dotted with pretty fishing villages and historic resorts such as Whitby and Scarborough.

SCARBOROUGH *above*

Scarborough was founded in 966 by the Viking raider Thorgils Skarthi. In 1626 Mrs Elizabeth Farrow found that the waters from a nearby stream had medicinal properties. She set off a chain reaction and people flocked to Scarborough Spa, Britain's first seaside resort. Anne Brontë, who had been suffering from consumption, visited with her sister Charlotte in the hope that the sea air would cure her. Sadly she died at the age of 28 and is buried in St Mary's churchyard. With its busier South Bay separated from the more tranquil North Bay by the Castle Headland, Scarborough has developed into the largest holiday resort on the Yorkshire coast.

HUMBER BRIDGE *below*

There have been numerous plans to span the Humber estuary: in 1872 a tunnel was proposed; in 1928 a multi-span truss bridge, and in 1959 a suspension bridge finally received approval. Construction began in 1973 and on completion in 1981 the 7282ft (2220m) bridge was the longest single-span suspension bridge in the world. Today the Humber Bridge is the world's fourth longest and more than 100,000 vehicles use it every week.

HAWORTH *left*

Set amid the bleak Pennine Moors above the Worth Valley, Haworth is inextricably linked with the Brontë name. The Reverend Patrick Brontë and his young family arrived in 1820 when he became the local vicar. The parsonage remained the family home for the rest of their lives and it was here that the sisters wrote their most famous novels: Charlotte's *Jane Eyre*, Emily's *Wuthering Heights* and Anne's *Agnes Grey* all appearing in 1847. The parsonage is now home to the Brontë Parsonage Museum and the Brontë Society. Another local attraction running through the village is the Keighley and Worth Valley Railway.

KILBURN WHITE HORSE *right*

The largest of Britain's 11 white horses, the Kilburn White Horse is cut into the hillside of Sutton Bank on the edge of the North York Moors, above the village of Kilburn. It was created in 1857 at the instigation of Thomas Taylor, a local resident, who was inspired by the white horse carved out of the Downs at Uffington in Oxfordshire. It took 33 men to cut the horse out of the hillside and six tonnes of lime were used to whiten the exposed rock. The white horse faces south-west and is clearly visible from many miles away, particularly from the east coast main railway line south of Thirsk.

BRADFORD *above*

In Norman times the original village of Bradford sprang up around the "broad ford" over the river now called the Bradford Beck. Since the 13th century textiles have been an important local industry, but the Industrial Revolution saw Bradford become world-famous for worsted cloth. The city thrived and developed an innovative manufacturing base. This innovation continues today, but the "dark satanic mills" have been replaced by high-tech, leisure, financial and service industries. In addition to the Leisure Exchange complex (foreground), Bradford also boasts the National Media Museum, one of the most visited museums outside London. The model industrial village of Saltaire is north of Bradford and was built by Sir Titus Salt to provide accommodation for the workers at his woollen mills.

SHEFFIELD *right*

From modest beginnings, Sheffield developed into a market town in the 13th century. By 1600 it had become the principal centre in England for the production of cutlery. Crucible steel was invented here in the 1740s, as was Sheffield plate, imitation silver plate made from copper sheet rolled between thin silver sheets. Surrounded by seven hills, Sheffield has 50 parks, five river valleys and two universities. It is remarkably green – one third of the metropolitan area lies within the Peak District National Park and the city has many sites of special scientific interest. Recently the city has re-positioned itself as a sporting and technology centre. The 25,000-seater Don Valley Stadium was built for the 1991 World Student Games, and is the largest athletics stadium in the UK.

YORK MINSTER *below*

The largest Gothic cathedral in northern Europe, York Minster soars above the city. The first church on the site is thought to have been built in haste in 627 for the baptism of Edwin, King of Northumbria. In the 13th century Archbishop Walter de Gray wanted a building to rival Canterbury cathedral. Building began in 1220 but it took 250 years to complete. The new cathedral was consecrated in 1472. The Minster is 485ft (148m) in length and each of the three towers is 196ft (60m) high. The Minster's stained-glass is remarkable: its Great East Window soars to 76ft (23.7m) and is the world's largest example of medieval stained-glass, while the famous Rose Window in the south transept celebrates the marriage of Henry VII to Elizabeth of York, uniting the royal houses of York and Lancaster.

CASTLE HOWARD *above*

Castle Howard is one of the grandest private houses in Britain. It has been home to the Howard family for over 300 years. The first phase of the house was built in Baroque style in the early 18th century by Sir John Vanburgh and Nicholas Hawksmoor for the third Earl of Carlisle. Around 1715 the Earl switched his attention to the design of the gardens and grounds. The west wing was completed a century later in contrasting Palladian style. In the 1,000 acres of beautiful gardens and grounds lie Vanburgh's Temple of the Four Winds and (foreground) the Castle Howard Mausoleum, designed by Hawksmoor. This is still the private burial place of the Howard family. In 1981 Castle Howard featured in the popular television adaptation of Evelyn Waugh's novel *Brideshead Revisited*.

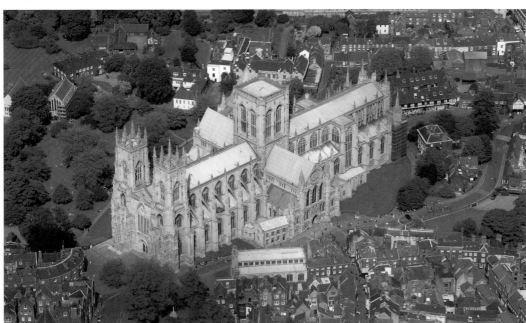

Northern England

North-west England stretches from Cheshire and the medieval walled city of Chester, to Lancashire, Cumbria and the Lake District. In the cities, the grime of the Victorian industrial era has been transformed. Today visitors come for the rich history and the regenerated city centres of Liverpool, European Capital of Culture in 2008, and Manchester. North-east England contains the bustling cities of Newcastle, Gateshead, Sunderland and Durham. To the north and west are the rolling hills and stunning coastline of Northumbria, with some of the most beautiful scenery in Britain.

Manchester Studios *above*

The television studios on Manchester's Quay Street were formerly known as Granada TV Studios. They are now owned by 3sixtymedia. They are still used for the filming of the UK's longest running television soap opera, *Coronation Street*. Corrie, as it is nicknamed, was first broadcast in December 1960. Between 1988 and 1999 fans flocked to the studios to visit the set and walk down the famous street, with its buildings built of reclaimed Salford brick. Weatherfield, the fictional suburb of Manchester where Coronation Street is based, was loosely based on Salford.

Salford Quays *right*

The cultural centre of Salford Quays sits on the site of the old Salford Docks on the Manchester Ship Canal. The docks closed in 1982 after a drastic slump in shipping hit the area hard. Millions of pounds have been spent on regeneration: in 2000 The Lowry Theatre and Art Gallery opened, named after the Salford artist LS Lowry, famous for his paintings of matchstick men in industrial settings. Across the water sits the shining Imperial War Museum North. Daniel Libeskind designed the building as a globe broken into three fragments, representing the devastating effects of war on the world. Linking the two is the Millennium lifting footbridge.

LIVERPOOL WATERSIDE *left*

Three buildings take pride of place at Pier Head. They are often referred to as Liverpool's Three Graces. The two largest clock-faces in Britain top the Liver Building's twin towers, built in 1911. It is still the head office of the Royal Liver Friendly Society. Next door is the Cunard Building, constructed between 1914 and 1917. It is irregular in shape – 30ft wider on the landside than on the waterside. Completing the trio is the Port of Liverpool Building, dating from 1907. Ferries still cross the river Mersey to Birkenhead, and now there are also two road tunnels under the river. The vibrant city of Liverpool is continually re-inventing itself. Much of the dock area and the city centre is in the process of regeneration. Liverpool has been designated European Capital of Culture 2008.

BLACKPOOL *below*

Still the UK's most popular seaside resort, the name Blackpool is derived from the black pool of water that flowed from a peat bog into the Irish Sea at this point. It first became known as a tourist resort in the 19th century. In its heyday, between 1900-1950, the beaches and promenade were crowded with factory workers from the north on their annual holiday. It is still the most popular holiday destination for Glaswegians. Today, Blackpool boasts more hotel and guesthouse beds than the whole of Portugal. Blackpool's famous tower was inspired by the Eiffel Tower. Constructed between 1897-1898, it stands 518ft (158m) high, and served as a radar station in the Second World War. It dominates the skyline and at its foot are bars, restaurants, the famous Tower Ballroom and Tower Circus. Close by, at the Winter Gardens, is the Opera House, one of Europe's biggest theatres. With miles of beaches and donkey rides during the summer months, Blackpool's attraction is timeless. One of the best ways to enjoy the extensive seaside promenade is to ride aboard the legendary trams which travel the 11-mile (18km) route between Starr Gate and Fleetwood. From August to November every year the bright light displays known as the Illuminations stretch along the seven miles (11km) of Blackpool's seafront.

CONISTON WATER *above*

Set back from the water's edge, the pretty village of Coniston sits at the foot of The Old Man of Coniston, at 2635ft (803m) one of the highest points in the Furness Fells. The Victorian poet, author and artist John Ruskin lived across the lake in Brantwood claimed that the view towards The Old Man of Coniston was "the best in all of England". Coniston Water is the third largest stretch of water in the Lake District, after Windermere and Ullswater. Here in 1939 Sir Malcolm Campbell set a world water speed record of 141.74mph (228.108kph) in his boat *Bluebird K4*. His son Donald tragically died on the lake in 1967 while attempting to exceed a speed of 300mph (483kph) in *Bluebird K7*. The name Bluebird lives on as the name of a beer brewed by the local Coniston Brewery.

PATTERDALE *left*

The village of Patterdale lies in the valley of the same name. It is the starting point for walks into the surrounding hills including the Striding Edge path up Helvellyn – a dramatic razor-sharp ridge famous among walkers and mountaineers. The renowned hill-walker and author Alfred Wainwright considered this his favourite valley in the Lakes because of its relatively unspoilt nature. To the south of Patterdale, the road to Ambleside leads over the Kirkstone Pass. At the top of the pass sits the Kirkstone Pass Inn, one of the highest pubs in England.

ULLSWATER *above*

Ullswater is often considered the most beautiful of the English lakes. It is the second largest lake in the Lake District at 7.5 miles (12km) long and three-quarters of a mile (1200m) wide, with three distinct bends that give it a dog-leg shape. Since 1855 steamers have connected the main centres on the lake: Glenridding to the south, Pooley Bridge to the north-east and Howtown halfway between. Tourists love this service as they can take a boat between Glenridding and Howtown and then walk back along some of the best low-level paths in the Lake District.

NEWCASTLE - BRIDGING THE TYNE

Both Newcastle and its close neighbour Gateshead across the river have a long history of shipbuilding and heavy industry. There has been a bridge at this point across the river Tyne since Roman times. Today there are no less than seven, from the Redheugh roadbridge furthest upstream, then the King Edward VII railway bridge and the Queen Elizabeth II metro bridge. Next is the High Level combined road and railway bridge just visible on the left of the photograph. Then comes the 1876 Swing Bridge and, to its right, soars the Tyne Bridge, a fine compression arch suspended-deck bridge, modelled on the Sydney Harbour Bridge. Finally (not pictured) the Millennium Bridge for cyclists and pedestrians, which opened in 2001. Nicknamed the "Blinking Eye", it tilts to allow small ships and boats to pass beneath. Echoing the curves of the nearby bridges, the shell-shaped Sage Gateshead (above) opened in 2004 as the quayside's latest addition to the skyline. It is Sir Norman Foster's first building dedicated to the performing arts and is home to the Northern Sinfonia orchestra. Just beyond the Sage and the Millennium Bridge is the Baltic Centre for Contemporary Art, converted from the former Baltic Flour Mills.

THE ANGEL OF THE NORTH *left*

Taller than four double-decker buses and with wings almost as wide as those of a Jumbo jet, Antony Gormley's Angel of the North attracts more than 150,000 visitors annually. The statue on a hillside outside Gateshead was completed in 1998; 65ft (20m) high and 175ft (54m) wide, it can be seen by drivers on the A1 and passengers on the east coast railway line. At first the Angel was controversial, but it is now very popular and has been classed as an "Icon of England" along with cricket and fish and chips!

HADRIAN'S WALL *above*

The Roman Emperor Hadrian ordered a great wall built of stone and turf to be erected after his visit to Britain in 122AD. At 13-15ft high and extending more than 70 miles (114km) west from Wallsend on the river Tyne to the Solway Firth, it was a huge effort of construction. The forts, temples, milecastles and turrets were manned by more than 10,000 troops. Hadrian's Wall does not mark the modern border but is located entirely in England. It is a World Heritage Site and one of northern England's most popular attractions.

WALES

Few countries have such a dramatic combination of mountain scenery, beautiful coastline, pretty villages and vibrant cities all within a relatively compact area. The ring of castles on the north and north-west coast are testament to the country's turbulent history. In the south the combination of coal and steel production powered the Industrial Revolution and quickened the growth of cities such as Cardiff and Swansea. In 2002 the Welsh Assembly was created – a powerful symbol of the resurgence of Wales.

CONWY *above*

The classic walled town of Conwy is guarded by 22 towers, and is dominated by its dark-stoned castle, now a World Heritage Site. Edward I built this fortress on the Conwy estuary in just six years, starting in 1283. It became one of his "iron ring" of castles, built to contain the Welsh. There are three parallel bridges crossing the estuary. Robert Stephenson's tubular railway bridge is furthest from the sea and was designed with mock fortifications at each end. Two further bridges for road traffic included the Conwy Suspension Bridge built by Thomas Telford in 1826. These days, the suspension bridge is the preserve of pedestrians, and all road traffic now crosses the river by tunnel. On the far side of the estuary is the town of Llandudno Junction.

CAERNARFON *left*

In a beautiful setting at the western end of the Menai Strait, Caernarfon is the largest Welsh-speaking community in Wales. But the legacy of English rule is evident. The magnificent castle with its 13 polygonal towers and impressive curtain walls was built close to the water's edge by Edward I in 1283, as a seat of power and a symbol of English dominance. Edward I proclaimed his son the first Prince of Wales at the castle in 1301. The investiture of a new Prince of Wales, held at Caernarfon Castle, is a relatively new idea, conceived by the local MP, David Lloyd George, and first held in 1911. The ceremony was again held on July 1 1969 at Caernarfon when Queen Elizabeth II invested her son Charles as Prince of Wales watched by 4,000 guests.

SNOWDONIA *left*

Yr Wyddfa, or Snowdon in English, is the highest mountain in England and Wales at 3560ft (1085m). The botanist Thomas Johnson made the first ever recorded ascent of Snowdon in 1639. On exceptionally clear days you can see Ireland, Scotland, England and Wales, as well as 24 counties, 29 lakes and 17 islands. Snowdon's six ridges each have their own special character. Those to the north and east are steep and rocky, and those to the south and west are grassy but more remote. There are seven main routes to reach the summit of Snowdon. They range from the easiest, the Llanberis Path or Tourist Path, to the toughest, the Snowdon Horseshoe. Most walkers take the Miners Track which skirts Llyn Glaslyn or Blue Lake at a height of 2200ft (670m). A more leisurely way to reach the summit is by the Snowdon Mountain Railway. This is Britain's only public rack and pinion railway. It climbs over 1000ft (305m) from Llanberis at an average speed of five miles per hour to the summit station at 3493ft (1065m).

HARLECH *right*

Seemingly growing out of the rock on which it sits and guards Snowdonia, Harlech Castle dominates the surrounding area. Edward I began building it in 1283 as one of his "iron ring" of fortresses to subdue the Welsh. Today the sea has retreated but the castle's massive inner walls and towers still stand. This is a truly formidable castle built in just seven years. Attackers faced daunting challenges: a sheer cliff-face rising from the sea and, on the landward side, the massive twin-towered gatehouse and concentric outer and inner walls. The Welsh leader Owain Glyndŵr captured the castle in 1404, and held a parliament there. Four years later Prince Henry (later Henry V) took it after a long siege. During the Wars of the Roses in 1468 its occupants surrendered after a seven-year siege – they were only able to resist for so long because they got supplies by sea. The siege inspired the ever-popular marching song *Men of Harlech*.

WORM'S HEAD *above*

Worm's Head is shaped like a giant sea serpent, which inspired Viking invaders to name it Wurm (meaning "dragon"). The headland forms the most westerly point of the Gower Peninsula – and the most photographed. The mile-long promontory is joined to the mainland by a rocky causeway, which is only exposed for two-and-a-half hours at low tide. Each part has its own name: the large flat-topped Inner Head, the natural rock bridge called Devil's Bridge, Low Neck and the Outer Head, a breeding ground for kittiwakes, herring gulls, guillemots and razorbills.

PORT TALBOT *left*

This was once a small port and market town called Aberafan, or Aberavon in English, which belonged to the medieval Lords of Afan. The Talbot family re-named it Port Talbot in the middle of the 19th century. Built along the eastern rim of Swansea Bay in Glamorgan in south Wales, Port Talbot is today a busy industrial town and harbour. The town is dominated by the Port Talbot Steelworks, originally part of British Steel, subsequently Corus, and which now belong to Tata Steel of India.

CARDIFF *above*

A small town until the early 19th century, Cardiff became a city in 1905 and the capital of Wales in 1955. During the 19th century, Cardiff's port – known as Tiger Bay – was one of the world's busiest. Today, Wales' largest city is a major centre of culture, sport, finance and business services; the magnificent new building, designed by Sir Richard Rogers for the National Assembly for Wales, houses the recently devolved government, built close to Cardiff Bay. Nearby is the Wales Millennium Centre, a stunning arts and entertainment complex. In the city centre is the Millennium Stadium, the national stadium of Wales, a popular venue for sport and music.

SEVERN BRIDGES *below*

The original Severn Bridge was opened in 1966 and the Second Severn Crossing, three miles downstream, in 1992. The new bridge, more than three miles (5km) long carries the M4 in a direct route from England to Wales. Tolls are charged on both, but only when travelling west.

RHONDDA VALLEY *above*

The view above is close to Porth, "the gateway to the Rhondda", which lies at the entrance to the two Rhondda valleys, the Rhondda Fach (little Rhondda) and the Rhondda Fawr (large Rhondda). This was once a sparsely populated area of great natural beauty, but the arrival of the railway in the middle of the 19th century brought the coal industry. Coalmining was to dominate the lives of the people and the landscape of the Rhondda valley for the next 150 years.

SCOTLAND

There is much more to Scotland than the two large cities of Edinburgh, Glasgow and the Highlands. This vast country includes 162 islands. Unst, in the Shetlands, is the most northerly inhabited Scottish island and it is nearer to Bergen in Norway than to Aberdeen. Rivalry between the Scots and the English is intense, particularly when it comes to sport. It is the legacy of both countries' history: Scotland is littered with battle sites where Scots and English troops fought for control over the centuries. The Acts of Union of 1707 finally united the two peoples under the Kingdom of Great Britain. With devolution in 1998 Scotland regained political control over its education, health and other regional issues. The magnificent new Parliament building in Edinburgh, designed by the Catalan architect Enric Miralles, opened in 2004.

GLASGOW *above*

By the end of the 19th century Glasgow was the second city of the British empire with a strong shipbuilding industry and a port trading in tobacco, sugar and cotton. Most of the world's locomotives and ships were built on the Clyde, and many famous ships, such as the *Queen Mary*, *Queen Elizabeth* and the former royal yacht *Britannia*. After the Second World War Glasgow's traditional industries such as shipbuilding were no longer viable and the city went into a slump. But a conscious cultural renaissance was rewarded with the status of

SOLWAY FIRTH *above*

Famous for its beautiful vistas and fast incoming tides, the Solway Firth forms the western border between England and Scotland which was established in law by the Treaty of York in 1237 and is one of the oldest borders in the world. The Solway Firth stretches from St Bees Head near Whitehaven in Cumbria to the Mull of Galloway in Dumfries. Numerous small ports, harbours and towns dot the intricate coastline of the Firth.

BEN NEVIS *right*

Britain's highest mountain, known locally as the Ben, is the 4406ft (1344m) Ben Nevis. It was first climbed in 1771 by the Edinburgh botanist James Robertson. When the poet John Keats reached the summit 47 years later, he compared the experience of climbing the Ben to "mounting ten St Pauls without the convenience of a staircase". Today there are about 100,000 ascents a year, mostly via the pony track from Glen Nevis.

LOCH LOMOND *below*

As the cloud lifts, the waters of Loch Lomond are revealed. This is the UK's largest stretch of fresh water, 24 miles (39km) long by five miles (8km) wide. There are about 38 islands in the loch, which is overlooked by the 3194ft (974m) mountain Ben Lomond. The loch is the jewel in the crown of the Loch Lomond and Trossachs National Park which was created in 2002 and contains some of Scotland's finest scenery. The park boasts no fewer than 20 Munros – mountains over 3000ft (914m).

LOCH NESS *above*

Loch Ness is the deepest of the Scottish lochs, and the second largest by surface area after Loch Lomond. It stretches about 23 miles (37km) between Fort Augustus in the south and Lochend in the north. The Great Glen Way runs from Fort William to Inverness. This 73 mile route follows the course of the Caledonian Canal along the shores of Loch Lochy, Loch Oich and Loch Ness. Walkers may hope to catch sight of Nessie, the legendary monster who reputedly inhabits the waters of Loch Ness.

European Capital of Culture in 1990 and Glasgow is now a dynamic centre for business and tourism. The former Queen's Dock, on the north bank of the Clyde, is now the Scottish Exhibition and Conference Centre. Part of this complex is the Armadillo – more formally called the Clyde Auditorium – a 3,000-seater concert venue which opened in 1997. Across the river the Glasgow Science Centre is a major tourist attraction. Next door is the Science Mall with three floors of over 300 hands-on scientific exhibits and the Scottish Power Space Theatre planetarium, a gleaming titanium building.

EDINBURGH *below*

Capital of Scotland since 1437, Edinburgh has been the seat of the new Scottish Parliament since devolution in 1998. As a World Heritage Site it attracts 13m tourists each year, making it the UK's second most visited city. Edinburgh Castle vies with Kelvingrove Art Gallery and Museum in Glasgow for the title of Scotland's most visited attraction. The castle dominates the city from its perch on Castle Rock. Most of it dates from the 16th century, though St Margaret's Chapel was built in the 12th century and is Edinburgh's oldest building. Every day except Sunday, the one o'clock gun booms over the city, a practice originally begun to provide a reliable time check for ships in the Firth of Forth. The arena with the blue seating next to the castle is used by military bands for the Edinburgh Military Tattoo. This is part of the three-week Edinburgh International Festival held in August every year. Alongside the main festival's programme of classical music, theatre and opera, the Edinburgh Festival Fringe showcases alternative and experimental works. Across the Princes St Gardens runs Princes Street, one of Edinburgh's main shopping thoroughfares.

URQUHART CASTLE *above*

The early history of Urquhart Castle on Loch Ness is unclear. It was captured by Edward I of England in 1296 and last saw action in 1689 when a garrison of supporters of William and Mary fought off troops loyal to James II. Three years later the castle was blown up.

FORTH BRIDGES *below*

By 1760 the ferry across the Firth of Forth was Scotland's busiest service but it was slow and sometimes dangerous. It was finally replaced in 1964 by the Forth Road Bridge (foreground). Just over 1.5 miles (2.5km) long from end to end, the Forth Road Bridge was Europe's longest suspension bridge when it opened. The Forth Railway Bridge was opened in 1890. It was one of the world's first steel bridges, requiring 54,000 tonnes of steel and 4000 men to drive home 6.5 million rivets! The painting of the bridge was a never-ending job, but the paint used today is designed to last 20 years.

First published in 2009 by
Myriad Books Limited
35 Bishopsthorpe Road, London
SE26 4PA

Photographs copyright
© Flight Images

Text copyright
© Graham Pritchard
Graham Pritchard has asserted his right under the Copyright, Designs and Patents Act 1998 to be identified as the author of this work.
All rights reserved. No part of this publication may be reproduced, stored on a retrieval system, or transmitted in any form or by any means, electronic, mechanical, photocopying, recording or otherwise, without the prior permission of the copyright owners.
ISBN 1 84746 239 1
EAN 978 1 84746 239 8

Designed by Jerry Goldie
Graphic Design

Printed in China

www.myriadbooks.com